T0158957

First LOVE

KELVIN WOODARD

WestBow Press books may be ordered through booksellers or by contacting:

WestBow Press
A Division of Thomas Nelson & Zondervan
1663 Liberty Drive
Bloomington, IN 47403
www.westbowpress.com
1 (866) 928-1240

ISBN: 978-1-5127-9550-9 (sc)
ISBN: 978-1-5127-9549-3 (e)

Library of Congress Control Number: 2017910980

Print information available on the last page.

WestBow Press rev. date: 10/05/2017

To my grandfather, affectionately known as "Deac," officially, Deacon Forest Johnson. Job 1:1 says, "And that man was perfect and upright, and one that feared God, and eschewed evil." This scripture is the only thing and the only example I've ever known of my grandfather. Some have called this a poem, but these are the words given to me by the Holy Spirit, recited and read at his funeral, entitled "Shoes." With permission, I placed a pair of his shoes on the podium and began to read the following:

Shoes

Forest Johnson, my grandfather, he wore a size-eleven shoe. I wore a size twelve, yet his shoes were too big for my feet. At the end of his journey here on earth, he was bound by a wheelchair, yet he stood taller than any man I know.

I can't tell you of all the places these shoes traveled, I can't tell you how rough the road, how tedious the journey or how long the path, but I do know that their steps were ordered by the Lord. These shoes walked some lonely roads, stood in some lonely places, not because there were no people around, but because they were shod with the preparation of the gospel of peace.

These shoes did not have secret rendezvous with strange women, they couldn't be found in a club or a bar, nor would they be seen in the halls of deceit. These shoes came home at night.

They were found at work early in the morning, many times before the break of day. They were not slothful; they didn't make excuses and stayed true to their word.

I had to come to the understanding that the size of a man was not measured in feet and inches but in the character in which he lived. My admiration for him was not for the things he had but for the word he lived. These shoes climbed the rough side of the mountain so that I wouldn't have to. They took a journey on a road less traveled so that my journey could be easier. These shoes didn't walk in the counsel of the ungodly, nor did they stand in the way of sinners or sit in the seat of the scornful.

These shoes were patient and kind; they were not easily provoked, were not puffed up, but delighted in the ways of the Lord. Whenever there was a church service, these shoes would be found ten to twenty minutes early. They didn't believe in being late, didn't care to be seen, just wanted to be at their appointed place.

And on that faithful Saturday evening, he heard the voice of the Lord call his name, saying, "Son it's time to come home. It's time for you to rest. Well done, my good and faithful servant. Enter into the joy of your Lord. You've fought a good fight. You've finished the course. You've kept the faith."

And as he stretched forth his hand to take that step from mortal to immortality, I can hear the Lord saying, "You can't come up here with those shoes on. You're going to have to take them off, for the ground you stand on is holy ground. Leave the shoes behind as a memorial to all that would see them so that they will know you walked with me until you were not."

For a man this great should leave shoes too big for the feet of the generations that would follow. He did not leave material wealth, for his treasure was stored in heaven above, which money could not buy. But what he did leave was a wealth of faith, perseverance, long-suffering, gentleness, meekness, and kindness, a wealth of truthfulness, integrity, wisdom, honor, and strength.

The story of these shoes can't end here; these shoes must continue to tell the story of a man who spent his life faithfully in the service of the God for whom he put his trust. These shoes can't be filled by the feet of one person alone, but if these shoes will walk again, it's going to take the feet of every family member to come together, despite differences and past dealings, if once again to show forth the greatness of the man that stood in them.

He was a man of few words who didn't waste time talking about what he was going to do—he just did it. And in the words of Benjamin Franklin, "Well Done is better than well said."

Well done, Granddad. Well done, our patriarch and our Isaac, Forest Johnson, "Deac," husband, father, grandfather, great-grandfather, great-great grandfather, uncle, brother-in-law, friend.

From all of us to you, thank you for leaving shoes.

In Loving Memory of Minnie D. Woodard

All my life I've known my mother as a woman of God who lived a life of holiness and walked upright before him. I've never known her to curse, lie, cheat, steal, or do anything that would displease God. She's the reason my father is saved and pastoring now. She's the reason my brothers and sister and I are saved. My mother intentionally lived holy before us every day. For some, good would have been good enough, or moral or even ethical, but she lived and showed us we can live holy also. There is no enumerating the impact she has had on my life. She was more than just a good mother; she was a son of God in the body of a woman named Minnie D. Woodard.

You have given me the greatest gift and the greatest advantage that creation and the world has ever known. I honor you and I thank you for giving me God.

Your son,
Kelvin Woodard

Contents

Foreword

Having grown up in church, I've heard many terms, phrases, scripture, quotes, and inspirational sayings, and for the most part, my understanding of their meanings was only on the surface, I had no real revelation of my own of their deeper meanings. I find that this is the case even today for much of the church membership. My inquiry in the word has led to much dialogue in the spirit, which in turn resulted in much (not to say I have more than any other) revelation in the spirit. One of those sayings is "I love him because he first loved me." Somehow my surface understanding of this phrase and the ensuing dialogue in the spirit led to the revelation revealed in this book.

In order to validate my surface understanding of that phrase, that it is not my understanding alone but that of a larger audience, I took an anonymous survey of twelve simple questions that every confessed Christian should know. Ten of the questions have simple yes-or-no answers, but two of the questions require a short answer. I must admit that I masked the true intent of the survey with the other ten questions when in reality the two short answer questions were the real reason for the survey. The two questions were as follows: What does "I love him because he first loved me" refer to, and what is the physical evidence/action/event in the Bible of this love?

It's funny how people are on guard when asked questions about their faith and what they believe. They tend to immediately look for the question within the question as if there is an alternative motive behind it or as if they are trick questions.

First of all, there is no right or wrong answer, the survey is to validate if my understanding is the same as the Christian church community at large. I believe that anyone professing Christianity should have come to the same general answer and every respondent answered the same way with the same scripture reference—a reference to the events of the crucifixion, as I expected. Now we will take a journey to uncover the question "What does 'I love him because he first loved me' mean?" and the referenced biblical evidence/action/event that gave rise to this book. I believe that we should question everything we read in the Bible. Not for the purpose of questioning its validity but to question it for revelation and understanding and pursue it until it is settled in our spirit. But the word cannot be revealed with our mind, our thinking, our reasoning, it must be revealed by the spirit. After all, the word is spirit and life and only the spirit of God can reveal the things of God. According to 1 Corinthians 2:14, "But the natural man receiveth not the things of the Spirit of God: for they are foolishness unto him: neither can he know them, because they are spiritually discerned."

The Mind of the Author

While listening to a sermon, the minister referred to the scripture in Philippians 4:6, "Be careful for nothing; but in everything by prayer and supplication with thanksgiving let your requests be made known unto God." While meditating on this scripture, the following conversation between the spirit and me ensued and went something like this.

The question from the spirit: "When does a person say thank you."

My response: "When they have received something."

And the spirit replied, "Right."

In the context of thanking God by faith for the things we petition, a sincere thank-you—even when we can't see, hold, touch, or physically possess it—is the only evidence that we believe we have received what we ask. Because faith is the substance of things "hoped" for, past tense, already received. I do not say thank you unless I believe or have received, seen, or held in my hand the thing I desire.

This is the same kind of dialogue during a time of meditation that led to this book. I do not remember what prompted the thought. I do remember asking the question, why heaven and earth, why this life, and why does all of this exist? Let's explore.

Acknowledgments

I would like to thank the Holy Spirit for prompting this in my spirit. That's not to make me seem spiritual, but I have never seen myself as an author of a book, nor would I have stepped out on this without believing it to be God inspired. It may not be groundbreaking, but I believe it would help put in perspective holiness and why it's required.

It is no wonder the world can't make heads or tails out of Christianity. We're all over the map, and if we're speaking to the same God, then someone is confused. I'll let you guess who's the guilty party.

I must thank God for the courage, inspiration, and revelation that he has given me to write this book. Until recently I did not see God using me in this capacity. I am humbled and thankful that he has. This is the revelation that was revealed to me, and we will soon find out if it was meant to remain with me or to be shared.

Chapter 1

WHY THE BEGINNING?

When Did He First Love Me? The Reason for Creation

Growing up with Sunday school and throughout most of my early Christian life, there was a song we used to sing. It went something like this:

There is a name I love to hear
I love to sing/hear God's word
It sounds like music to my ear
The sweetest name on earth
Oh, how I love Jesus
Oh, how I love Jesus
Oh, how I love Jesus
Because he first loved me

This book is an excerpt of the thoughts and wonderings of my mind in questioning the phrase and asking what we mean by "because he first loved me." In order to add validity to the purpose or the revelation revealed to me on this subject, I began to ask the body—the body of Christ, people of faith, people in churches, professed Christians—this question. The overwhelming majority answered as I had expected. That was when I knew that this book would be a tool to help open the understanding and even cause us to challenge and see the Bible and events in the Bible from a different focal point.

I'm not saying that I had to write this book for the sake of the people's understanding. There is not to my knowledge an urgency or emergency for this book. But I do believe there is a need in the body for a greater revelation of God's word. Having said that, I am not making this book out to be that revelation. That's my disclaimer.

Back to the question of "What does it mean?" I remember thinking about the role time plays in validating the statement "because he first loved me," for me, by the majority thought and accepted belief that Jesus came and died for us some four thousand years after the Genesis 1:1 "in the beginning." I thought that was just too long to show someone that you love him or her.

After compiling the answers, other questions began to emerge, like could Moses make the statement "because he first loved me?" Could Joshua, Isaac, Ruth, or Joseph make that statement? We have the physical proof in the New Testament of God showing his love for humankind. In John 3:16, he gives his life in one of the most horrific kinds of deaths imaginable, and he does so of his own free will. He had every ability and power to avoid not just the death but also the excruciating pain, torture, and agony that came with it. So I see why we sing the song, because we have the New Testament, but it took four thousand years. Where is the evidence of God's love before that? Where is the physical evidence that he loved us before his son died on the cross?

Most of you right now are probably citing numerous examples in the Old Testament: the promises to Abraham, Daniel in the lions' den, the Hebrew boys, Joseph, David, the Exodus, Elijah, Ruth, and Naomi, and so on. And you're right. But those are individual stories/ situations that yes, show God's love toward his people and chronicle Israel's journey over time, but where is the I-love-humankind event in the Old Testament?

I suspect that the remainder of the content in this book will probably be controversial at first glance if explanation is not allowed. Some may even say sacrilege. I ask that you listen to the argument and the supporting scripture before passing judgment. I admit I have never heard anyone bring out the concepts that I am about to bring forth in this reading. Before I go on, this is not an attempt to bring a new concept or any form of condemnation, just a revelation. Nor is it intended for sensationalism or radicalism. I myself am very cautious when I hear someone with a revelation that no one else has had or even spoken of, especially knowing the many renowned authors, teachers, and preachers of the word, both past and present. To be honest about it, the word doesn't specifically state what I am about to say. It would have to be inferred and probably does not work without allowing the concept or theory I am about to introduce. I realize that makes it self-serving, but I believe both theories are solid. Of course, you will judge their validity.

Two questions, two theories, two events. The answers to these will take us on a journey of discovery that will open our spiritual understanding to the importance of the call of discipleship—why we must live a holy life before God and maybe even bring into question the acceptance of some practices in the church. Questions: Why is there a heaven and earth? What is the evidence that he first loved us (humankind)? Theories: why one stops when pursuing something and the model of man. Events: creation itself and ending the creation with Eve.

Why Is There a Heaven and Earth?

Why heaven and earth? Years ago I taught the concept that I'm about to explain to you. I titled it "The Parable of Heaven and Earth." Let's investigate, but before we do, I must bring in a concept that I created. I'm not trying to give myself credit for this—just trying to set the record straight that to my knowledge there is no scientific term, word, or phrase for this theory. I will call it *the law of the end of pursuit*. I have googled the term and have not found anything comparable to the concept, so I feel a level of confidence that I am not taking someone else's term or phrase.

There is a law enforcement term that deals with pursuit, but this one really deals with the end of the pursuit. It simply states that the reason a pursuer stops pursing a thing is the thing that is pursued has been attained. Why did the lion stop chasing the deer? Because he caught it. Why did the doctor stop going to med school? Because he got his degree. And what was the last thing they did before they stopped? They attained the thing they pursued. The event that took place just before they stopped is the indicator of their reason, their intent, or their desire from the beginning. Back to my parable of heaven and earth, this is a summary of the lesson and the objective thereof.

To set the scene in the parable, think of an early man sitting in a cave and about to take his first foray into the discovery of the wonders of outdoors. Each day he discovers something new. One day it's water. Another, fire. He discovers minerals in the earth and the components for marble, iron, textiles, stone, cement, rock, and the building material of trees, such as paper and wood. He discovers gas and oil and their benefits. So we follow the humans through their discovery journal. But we wonder, "Are these discoveries isolated incidents, or do they lead to some greater purpose?" He puts one and one together and builds on the knowledge that he has gained over time through experiment and trial and error that result in his building this structure.

Dream house, Home, Luxury Mansion, Success

And with all the knowledge he has gained that gave him the ability to build this, the ability to manufacture and construct highways, vehicles, machines, buildings—anything his heart desires—he never builds anything else. Why does he stop when there is so much potential before him? Because all of that discovery, learning, experience, and ability culminated in the reason he started in the beginning. He wanted to build himself a house, which was the thought in his mind from the beginning, before he took his first walk.

In this example, because of man's limited knowledge of the future, his desire to build a house came only after his knowledge and ability of discovery. This leads to gathering the material needed to construct/assemble/manufacture the house. The difference with creation is God didn't go through a discovery process. He had and has always had all knowledge from the beginning. What man discovered, God had already provided for in creation. Now parallel the details of creation and notice when God finished the creation process. Why all the plants, animals, gardens, trees, waters—all of the elements that God placed in the earth that have sustained humans from the beginning? What completed the dream? What was the last thing created that signaled the very thought that started the "Let there be light"? It was the creation of Eve.

So what does Eve represent? Physically and naturally, she was the wife of Adam, because it was not good that Adam (man) should be alone. Adam just so happened to be modeled after God himself. God made man in his likeness and his image. He (God) by default is now the model for man; therefore, the statements that he made about man in the beginning in theory became statements that he made about himself. The specific statement referred to is in Genesis 2. "It is not good that man should be alone." Based on this theory, that verse would be restated to say, "It is not good that I (God) should be alone.

The Bible says he changes not. He knows the end from the beginning, and he is omniscient, omnipresent, and omnipotent. As you read the Bible, you will discover that God does not start anything unless he has first finished it. It's like looking at a sign saying, "Coming soon," with a picture of an office high-rise standing on the ground of an empty rock-and-weed-filled lot. God sees our finish when all we can see is our brokenness. Before God said, "Let there be light," he saw mankind, the body of Christ, the bride of Christ, and the marriage supper. So, because he saw his bride before there ever was he created provision for his bride in mortality through eternity. In so doing he provided for man's eternity before he provided for his mortality. Therein he created heaven and earth, and sacrificed a lamb before the foundation of the world that his bride will be with him through eternity.

> And he saith unto me, Write, Blessed are they which are called unto the marriage supper of the Lamb. And he saith unto me, these are the true sayings of God. (Revelation 19:9)
>
> Come hither, I will shew thee the bride, the Lamb's wife. (Revelation 21:9)

These words/thoughts weren't just part of the end of the Bible—Revelation. These are the thoughts of God before he said, "Let there be light."

The Case for Holiness

Be ye holy as I am holy. Everyone is ok; everyone is going to heaven. First holiness was the standard, then morality as defined by man. I remember watching a talk show on television some years ago, and the host was saying how God would not punish sin in horrific ways, because he's a loving God. And I remember how the audience reacted to the statement with such agreement. Because their understanding of a loving God is that he would only do those things that are amenable to our senses or consciences.

the situation; he was looking at the end, the marriage supper. And although everyone would from that point on be born into sin and fall short of the glory of God, all would not remain in sin. Some would receive salvation and dedicate their lives, souls, hearts, and minds to him.

Yes, Adam and Eve would fall, but he saw you at the marriage table, and because he saw you, he said it is worth it, and your fall doesn't have to be your end, just a testimony of the power of God to overcome any and all obstacles, the power to be more than a conqueror. My son has prepared a body, to reconcile you back to me. I have you covered. See you at the marriage supper.

Without Spot or Wrinkle

> And there shall in no wise enter into it any thing that defileth, neither whatsoever worketh abomination, or maketh a lie: but they which are written in the Lamb's book of life. (Revelation 21:27)

> That he might present it to himself a glorious church, not having spot, or wrinkle, or any such thing; but that it should be holy and without blemish. (Ephesians 5:27)

He's talking about marriage, because this is what he requires of his bride, the church, the body of Christ: holiness. For years growing up in church, I've heard this scripture about "without spot or wrinkle," and I have always wondered how we would ever make it. Does he really expect us to be without spot or wrinkle? How on earth can we live that kind of life?

While preparing to teach on this very subject and asking God to give me a revelation, this is how the Holy Spirit presented it to me. How is a spot or wrinkle formed? Like most people, I said a stain is made by an unwanted or unintended spill on a surface. Webster describes it as a small area visibly different than the surrounding area.

A wrinkle would be an unwanted or unintended fold or crease in something, usually in a garment. As in life, any spill can be cleaned up if it is dealt with immediately. It's when we let it sit that it leaves a spot (stain).

Then the Holy Spirit began to say that a spot isn't so much a spill on the surface as much as it is a spill that is allowed to sit. That's when it becomes a stain, when nothing is done about it. So a spot in the spirit doesn't mean that we won't sin. It's when we sin and allow it to continue, when we don't take immediate steps to rid ourselves of the sin. It's the small foxes or little sins that we sometimes ignore.

So what causes a wrinkle? Just like the spot, it's unaddressed sin. The passage the spirit gave me for this is Matthew 5:23–24: "Therefore if thou bring thy gift to the altar, and there rememberest that thy brother hath ought against thee; Leave there thy gift before the altar, and go thy way; first be reconciled to thy brother, and then come and offer thy gift." These are situations in our lives we haven't ironed out, and much of them have to do with a reverse ideology of how we think instead of what the word says.

The part of this scripture that stood out to me is that it's incumbent upon me to reconcile with my brother if I know he has aught against me. Most of us look at it in the reverse and say that if he's the one with the problem, he should come to me. That's not what the Bible says. In the society we live in, this is not easy if you're the one at fault, but the Bible is clear that if you don't straighten it out, you are at fault.

Sure, your family, friends and loved ones will lead you to believe that you are in the right and you should stand your ground. Don't take the position of weakness. Our lives can fold through many situations, and we can address the sin with the Holy Spirit or hope that no one will know and just let it sit. The delayed answer is usually a heated iron at extreme temperatures. So we live most of our lives in the heat of correction.

I'd rather be between a rock and hard place than an iron and a hot place. Unfortunately, too much of the church membership live their lives cleaning spots and in the heat of ironing out wrinkles. We take grace for granted, in hopes of more time, allowing spots to take root making cleaning up that much more difficult and costly. Some spots/wrinkles, we let sit because we've been hurt. Sometimes we feel we have a right to have spots, because, "you don't know what they did to me."

Now that we have allowed the stains to become spots and the creases to become wrinkles, the measures we sometimes take to remove the blemishes do more damage to the garment, our spirit, than they do to correct the problem. Sometimes, because judgment is not swift and God continues to show his love and care for us, we can get a false since of security, believing that a little spot or wrinkle is ok, but it's not. He's coming back for a glorious church and won't be taking spots and wrinkles back with him, only cleaned garments, because a holy God requires a holy bride.

> He that loveth not knoweth not God; for God is love.
> (1 John 4:8)

God is love. It's his DNA, and therefore, everything he does toward his people is out of love, even when sometimes the internal situations may seem ugly.

So, why heaven and earth and what is the first physical evidence or event that showed he loves us? Short answer, because he wanted a bride and the creation of heaven and earth.

Chapter 2

LOVE, CREATION, AND THE SABBATH: A REMEMBRANCE NOT TO FORGET YOUR FIRST LOVE

In the previous chapter I explained that creation is the first physical sign of God's love toward us. After God created heaven and earth, Genesis 2:2–3, the Bible says, "And on the seventh day God ended his work which he had made; and he rested on the seventh day from all his work which he had made. And God blessed the seventh day, and sanctified it: because that in it he had rested from all his work which God created and made."

Have you ever been in love and remembered the day of the week you proposed, or she said she loves you and you celebrated that day of the week or date of the month as an anniversary? In Jewish literature, poetry, and music, Shabbat is described as a bride or queen. Exodus 20:8: Remember the sabbath day, to keep it holy. Exodus 31:14: Ye shall keep the sabbath therefore; for it is holy unto you: Exodus 31:15: Six days may work be done; but in the seventh is the sabbath of rest, holy to the Lord:

Here God commands an observance that we are to keep every week for the rest of our lives. He establishes the cyclic seven-day week and says for as long as you live do not let this cycle of life take place without resting. There is a term called the *Law of First Use*, and what it means is that when you see something done the first time, you in essence receive the purist meaning and intent of its use or existence. Notice there was no command in the beginning for man not to work on this day of rest—Sabbath, because man originally was not made to work until after the fall.

So what was the first original use, intent, and understanding of rest? Until we know that, we won't really understand the Sabbath beyond a day not to work, but to rest. In order to have a greater revelation of the Sabbath or a more complete understanding, let's take a look at Genesis 2:3. It reads, "And God blessed the seventh day and sanctified it for in it he rested." There are three words in this passage that first must be defined if we are to get any meaning out of this scripture at all. These three words define the *who*, *what*, *where*, *how*, and *why*.

The *when* is given in the fourth word that I will mention. It is of less importance but is made important because of what God decrees about it. The three words are *blessed*, *sanctified*, and *rest* or *rested*. The fourth word or phrase is *the seventh day* that is only made important because of what God decrees upon it. The Hebrew word for *blessed* used in this verse is made up of two words that mean "kneel" and "self," the perfect picture of personal/individual worship. In our Western English understanding, we interpret or translate the meaning as "blessed," but in this revelation of its Hebrew (original) meaning, it is interpreted as "worship."

Then he sanctified it, consecrated and dedicated, hallowed it out, made it holy. In doing so he sat it aside, made it special and put worship in a class all by itself. In essence, he is saying that worship catches my attention. In Exodus 31:14–15, it reads, "Ye shall keep the sabbath therefore; for it *is* holy unto you … but in the seventh ***is*** the sabbath of rest, holy to the LORD."

This Sabbath is holy to you and it's holy to me. The English word *rest* in this verse is "to celebrate," and the word *rested* in Hebrew means "special holiday." He says, "I want you to remember what I've done for you and how I've showed my love toward you in creation.

I'm seeking the true worshipper and when I find him it causes me to *shabath* (celebrate)."

I originally thought "the seventh" (the fourth word) was significant, but it isn't—it's just the day that he rested. It becomes important because of what he says about it. He blessed it and he sanctified it. The blessing and sanctifying becomes important when you understand why, because he wanted to celebrate what he had done, not the creation of heaven and earth, but the creation of "the bride." He wanted to celebrate is the very reason he said, "Let there be light."

So the Sabbath becomes a special day set aside (consecrated, made holy) to be observed every cycle of life where we celebrate God through worship. If I were to further translate it, I would call it the celebration of "holy matrimony." Do not allow this cycle of life (seven-day week) to go by without you celebrating/worshipping me. Don't forget your first love. (John 4:21: "Jesus saith unto her, 'Woman, believe me, the hour cometh, when ye shall neither in this mountain, nor yet at Jerusalem, worship the Father.'")

In the fulfilling of the law, it is not intended that we worship only on the seventh or on this mountain or in Jerusalem, but a true worshipper lives a life of worship. Have you ever been in love with a woman, or in worship of a woman, and you thought about her night and day. You didn't take a breath without thinking of her—at work, at the mall, every moment of the day. There was no special place you designated to think of her. Not only did you worship her on the mountain and in Jerusalem, but also you worshipped her in the mall, at work, on your way to work, in the kitchen. You thought about her before you went to bed and when you woke up in the morning.

Daniel lived such a life of worship until his enemies knew the only way to trap him was to do so by worship. Our worship is not confined to the Sabbath, but to our heart and love toward God.

Chapter 3

THE LAW: NOT DESTROYED, JUST FULFILLED

Over the years I've heard much about the Old Testament and the Law. There is a thought that the Old Testament is not valid for this New Testament (covenant) era, and the Law is done away with and does not apply.

"All scripture is given by inspiration of God, and is profitable for doctrine, for reproof, for correction, for instruction in righteousness" (2 Timothy 3:16). Jesus clearly said in Matthew 5:17, "Think not that I am come to destroy the law, or the prophets: I am not come to destroy, but to fulfil."

What is the fulfilling of the law? The law itself has no spirit; it was words on a tablet. It could not live, interpret, or give the revelation of its words. It could just present them, make them known. With Christ, the example he lived, and the Holy Spirit, the word can now live, come to life. We can receive the interpretation and revelation of the law beyond the words. The tablets are now a part of our lives, an inherent, inseparable part of us. We no longer have to consult a book or tablet to know what or what not to do. It is now as instinctive as breathing. It doesn't make us obey, but it does make us without excuse. God changes not and his words, intent, and thoughts are everlasting, just as the words of a king are lawful, binding, can't be changed, and live as long as the king does. The law is not destroyed, just the method by which we live them.

When you worship in spirit and in truth, you worship out of your heart and love for God and not by rules or obligation (law). Your heart obligates you. The truth will make you free, and it is only the spirit of God that reveals God and therefore reveals the truth of his word. The freedom of the revelation of truth is that I can worship God according to my heart and not according to rules.

I don't have to be, as Jesus called the Pharisees (the church of that day), "hypocrites" and pray aloud when I have an audience in order to look Christian or holy. Nor do I have to appear pious, with a sad countenance, a disfigured face, effete, or travailing when fasting to make the "right impression." I don't have to testify on the mountain while actually living in the basement to show that God is blessing me. I don't have to put on a face of "blessed and highly favored" when I'm really torn and broken and on the verge of a breakdown. I can come to him with the truth of who I am and where I stand. After all, how do you fool an all-knowing God? I can say that I don't know how to make the next step, and he will be my strength.

So I don't have to follow the traditions of man in order to please God. You can't tell me how to worship my God; my heart will. My worship may be ugly to you, but if it's the truth of my heart, it pleases God. This does not, by any means, give one carte blanche to do as one pleases, for all must be done decently and in order: "And if you're led in truth by the spirit it will make sure that it is also in line with the spirit of God" (1 Corinthians 14:40).

Exodus 21:24 says, "Eye for eye, tooth for tooth." In Matthew 5:38–39, Jesus references this scripture in the Old Testament and says, "But I say unto you, that ye resist not evil." This sounds like a contradiction of the Old Testament, kind of like Jesus's explanation of the Sabbath. He is the fulfillment of the word. After all, he is the word. He wrote the book.

> The woman saith unto him, Sir, I perceive that thou art a prophet. Our fathers worshipped in this

> mountain; and ye say, that in Jerusalem is the place where men ought to worship.
>
> Jesus saith unto her, Woman, believe me, the hour cometh, when ye shall neither in this mountain, nor yet at Jerusalem, worship the Father. Ye worship ye know not what: we know what we worship: for salvation is of the Jews. But the hour cometh, and now is, when the true worshippers shall worship the Father in spirit and in truth: for the Father seeketh such to worship him. God *is* a Spirit: and they that worship him must worship *him* in spirit and in truth. (John 4:19–24)

Here the woman makes a statement referencing the tradition of a specific designated place to worship, and Jesus corrects her and tells her how worship works in the spirit. He says neither in this mountain or in Jerusalem will you worship the Father. He's not saying that this mountain or Jerusalem is off limits for worship. He's saying that a true worshipper, one who worships in spirit and in truth, has no designated place to worship.

There is no law that says you only worship at church on Sunday, during a midweek service, or at a specific location or building. They will worship on the mountain, they'll worship in the valley, they'll worship when they're going through, and they'll worship at the house, on the job, in the mall, or wherever and whenever they think about his goodness. A true worshipper doesn't have to come to church on Sunday to get his or her praise on, because the praise and the spirit of the worshipper is not in a law or a place but on the table of our hearts.

Luke 6:31 says, "And as ye would that men should do to you, do ye also to them likewise." The point here is to do unto other as we would have them do unto us, not to do to them what they do to us.

The entire premise behind these laws is fairness. If you cause hurt, harm, danger, or loss, then restore in kind. The punishment is an eye for an eye, but the intent is not. Hopefully, if you know the punishment, you'll think twice before someone has to lose an eye.

In the chapter "When Did He First Love Me?" I talked about

how God does things with the end in mind. That's how the spirit works; its goal is the fulfillment of the intent of God. It does nothing for the moment—everything has a future outcome. That's why we must wait patiently and trust God, because what he is doing through us while we're going through will ultimately end for the good of his glory. One may even look at it as God's strategy.

Strategy is never for the moment, but for a future outcome. Jeremiah 29:11 says, "I know the thoughts I think toward you, to give you an expected end." That expected end is the process that God takes us through in the fulfilling the destiny and intent for which he created us.

Some years ago while preparing to teach a lesson the Spirit said, "He who gives the vision is the only one who can take you to the vision." We can't start this journey in God and end with our own thinking or ability. If it starts with the spirit, it must end with the spirit, not a set of rules. He is the author and finisher of our faith, not just the author or just the finisher. For without faith, it is impossible to please God. Romans 10:17, says, "Faith cometh by hearing and hearing by the word of God," all of his word. His old word and his new word, and all is made known or revealed by his Spirit. Paul says it like this in Romans 7:6, "But now we are delivered from the law, that being dead wherein we were held; that we should serve in newness of spirit, and not *in* the oldness of the letter."

His word is eternal and never dies. Remember one of the attributes of a king is that his word lives as long as he does, and, once spoken, cannot be changed. Think about it: the oldest living book ever and with all the changes, innovations, advances since in the beginning. There has never been an update, upgrade, or modification of his word, because the King's word lives forever. So, the fulfillment of the Law ends in accomplishing the intent of God, which must first come with an understanding or revelation by the Spirit in order to be carried out properly. That's what Jesus did in fulfilling the Law—he showed us how to properly administer, carry out the intent, and showed us the heart of God behind the tablets. Psalms 13:10 says it like this: "Love worketh no ill to his neighbour: therefore love is the fulfilling of the law."

Chapter 4

THE TRANSCENDING ATTRIBUTE OF ETERNITY

The Eternal Transcending Attributes of God

1. He has no beginning and has no end
2. He changes not
3. He knows the end from the beginning

Because of these three factors God's thoughts are eternal and therefore are, were, and will always be in effect, meaning, his thoughts (spirit/ intent) has always been with him and have always been in effect regardless of when spoken or vocalized.

As example; "Faith is the substance of things hoped for the evidence of things not seen as yet," spoken and found in the New Testament (Heb 11:1). But was true and in operation before he even said, "Let there be light," and throughout the Bible we see the evidence of Hebrews 11:1 thousands of years before we heard It in our ear. In Romans 10:17, the Bible says, "So then faith cometh by hearing, and hearing by the word of God." We hear this for the first time in Romans, but it was true and in operation throughout the Old Testament, and Hebrews, the eleventh chapter, recorded the acts of faith of Moses, Abraham, Enoch, Abel, Noah, David, and so on.

We read about tithing in Malachi, but the Bible said that Abraham paid a tithe to Melchizedek long before there was a command. God spoke it and it was recorded, but the thought was always with God.

The Spirit Has an Intent that Results in Righteousness

God, "with whom there is no variation or shadow of turning" (James 1:17), does not change (Malachi 3:6). The Israelites received two laws from Moses: the law of Moses, that of ordinances and ceremonies; and the law of God, embodied in the Ten Commandments, which is an expression of God's character. If God does not change, neither will His Law. "My covenant I will not break, nor alter the word that has gone out of My lips" (Psalm 89:34). "I know that everything God does will endure forever; nothing can be added to it and nothing taken from it" (Ecclesiastes 3:14). "The works of his hands are faithful and just; all his precepts are trustworthy. They are steadfast for ever and ever, done in faithfulness and uprightness" (Psalm 111:7, 8).

The Bible gives a detailed accounting of the creation of earth but only tells us that in the beginning God created heaven and earth. There are other scriptures that describe heaven, but none detail its creation. We know that through the tempting of Eve, Satan was on earth in the form of a snake, which meant that his fall had already taken place. So the time span from the creation of heaven to Lucifer's fall from grace to become Satan and the "in the beginning" of the creation of earth, there is no knowing. It would be pointless anyway. We wouldn't know how to measure it, because there was no such thing as time. Heaven existed in the infinite as it does today.

In creation we see the priority or hierarchy of how God creates. He created provision before he created the purpose of the creation. All of creation was made to provide for man, his body, his bride. That's why he certified every aspect of creation with "and he saw that it was good." He created provision forever for his bride, both in mortality (earth) and in eternity (heaven, and access through his being slain before the foundation of the world). Since "in the beginning," he has never had to go back and make more provision. Man was not an afterthought; he was *the* thought. God has no need for earth and its provision, or for heaven, for that matter. Man can never say that he was ever without provision, body, soul, or spirit.

Chapter 5

THE BODY OF CHRIST: A PARALLEL ANATOMY

In the Bible, the phrase "body of Christ" is mentioned to show how all believers together make one body, fitly joined together—how each of us needs all of us, what affects one affects all, a three-Musketeers approach to how all believers should act toward each other, an all-for-one-and-one-for-all belief.

There are other analogies that could be made other than that of a body, but the word chose to use this term. In order to begin to understand the scope of the analogy, a study into the interactions and functions of the body is warranted. What does the phrase "body of Christ" tell us about how we should treat, respect, encourage, lift up, bind together, and love each other as brothers and sisters in Christ?

In school we are taught about the different systems of the body, such as the circulatory, respiratory, skeletal, and so on, their functions, how they support each other, their purposes and importance. I will spare you the series of lessons on each of the different systems. Instead, I want to make a spiritual comparison of how we, the body of Christ, should act and interact with each other.

The Skin

As it relates to the body, the only part of the body that most people will ever see is our skin. They don't get to see our internal organs. This skin becomes the face of Christ to the world. It is formed and shaped by the different systems of the body, which is manifested in the unique structure that distinguishes us from each other. As fearfully as God has made us, technically all we ever see of each other is skin. It is the face of Christianity that the world sees. The skin replenishes itself thirty thousand to forty thousand cells per minute. It replenishes itself because it loses skin cells at the rate of tens of thousands a minute. That skin becomes dust, and as the word says in Genesis 3:19, "In the sweat of thy face shalt thou eat bread, till thou return unto the ground; for out of it wast thou taken: for dust thou art, and unto dust shalt thou return."

That dead skin (dust) represents those saints who have passed, for it is the only physical evidence of their remains/existence, a kind of circle of life. Sometimes this skin, this face of Christianity, experiences trauma that, depending on the source, has two opposing goals.

Trauma: To Destroy or to Heal

We have all experienced some form of trauma in our lives, whether it was constructive as in surgical to repair, or destructive as in a stab, gunshot wound, or accident. In either case, the body acts the same to heal and repair. Let's take a look at the spiritual connotation behind this trauma, its result, and the actions the body takes to heal itself. We will look at how God addresses it and then at how we should address it in the context of what takes place in real life when the body experiences trauma.

Destructive trauma, we will call an attack on the body. Most people will agree that a stab, gunshot wound, cancer, some deadly disease, or intentional blunt-force trauma is designed to destroy the body. This attack we'll further define as sin, because that's exactly what sin is designed to do, destroy the spiritual body of Christ. Let's take a look at a few examples in the Bible.

In Numbers 16, starting at the first verse, it tells of Kohath, Dathan, and Abiram, who defy or question Moses's leadership, and in the thirty-first through the thirty-third verses, the earth opens up and swallows them, their households, and all of those who followed them. This sin, this attack against the body, this rebellion against leadership that God had put in place, was a destructive trauma that God surgically removed, kind of like a cancer. Although they were the core of the sin, God also removed the mass that surrounded them (those who aligned themselves with them).

Even though he removed the cancer, surgery still left a scar. Some scars are in places that we cover with clothing and keep hidden from the world, scars we mask with words of faith we dare to live, statements of victory that we don't believe. Some scars are in places the world can visibly see. They both remind us of God's grace, mercy, sovereignty, and judgment. They are reminders to us of the cost of sin.

In Joshua 7, the children of Israel were given instructions in battle to destroy everything and not take any spoils. Achan decided he wanted some gold for himself. After all, who would know? The twenty-fourth through twenty-sixth verses read as follows:

> And Joshua, and all Israel with him, took Achan the son of Zerah, and the silver, and the garment, and the wedge of gold, and his sons, and his daughters, and his oxen, and his asses, and his sheep, and his tent, and all that he had: and they brought them unto the valley of Achor. And Joshua said, Why hast thou troubled us? the LORD shall trouble thee this day. And all Israel stoned him with stones, and burned them with fire, after they had stoned them with stones. And they raised over him a great heap of stones unto this day. So the LORD turned from the fierceness

> of his anger. Wherefore the name of that place was called, The valley of Achor, unto this day.

Here in this passage we see that God allowed the children of Israel to exact the punishment for sin. That great heap of stones in the twenty-sixth verse is the scar that is a memorial, a sort of spiritual scab and a constant reminder of the cost of sin. That cancer he did not heal or apply spiritual chemotherapy to. He surgically removed it, and it became dust.

Most Christians and nonbelievers alike know the story of Jonah. Here Jonah sins in disobeying God's instructions and thinks by trying to run he can escape, as if God's word was optional for him. As in the case of Achan, God could have dealt with Jonah in the same manner, but he chose to rehabilitate Jonah. Oftentimes during the rehabilitation period, we can feel alone, as if we are out to sea without a paddle. This is an example of a constructive trauma. And it is a constant reminder of God's grace toward us.

Destructive trauma is sin designed to destroy; constructive trauma is God's response to that destructive trauma to make the body whole again, either through the surgical removal or surgical repair of the source. Sometimes this process seems more real than a physical traumatic event. Whether constructive to remove or to repair, the result is the same: to make the body whole. The difference is that one surgically removes the source of the sin and the other, because of the pliability of the heart, surgically repairs the source. At any rate the surgery leaves a scar as a reminder.

Further, we can see examples of either constructive trauma to heal or destructive trauma to destroy in how God dealt with David's son for David's sin. In Acts 5, we see Ananias with Sapphira, lying to the Holy Ghost. They are not given another chance, God surgically removed that sin. Peter denies Christ and is given the opportunity to "feed my sheep."

How the Body Heals Itself: The Blood's Reaction

In researching to understand the revelation of "the body" of Christ, I was led to find out what actions the body takes automatically, instinctively, without thought when the body is under attack. Usually this attack is from external sources and affects the body by destroying organs, functionality, immediately beginning to degrade capabilities and effectiveness. The body can suffer a break or a tear in the skin through such events as blunt force trauma that can take place in an assault or in a car accident. The body can also suffer a traumatic event by stabbing or gunshot wounds. This would be characterized as destructive trauma. Whether accidental or not, they immediately put the body or life in danger. Regardless of how, the body immediately takes steps to save itself or give itself the chance to be saved.

In the army we rehearsed immediate action drills and battle drills; they were designed to give us the best chance at survival under certain situations. We rehearsed them to the point that they became instinctive, part of an automatic response, because in war there are some situations soldiers may be subjected to that thinking about what to do may take too long to save their lives. One must react without thought, in much the same way as our body does.

I will explain the process the body takes automatically in six steps to make it easier to follow.

Step 1. At the moment a tear or puncture in the skin or body is made, the life-saving process that our body takes immediately and automatically begins. During this process, blood vessels tighten to reduce blood flow to the affected area.

Step 2. A plug is formed, causing blood vessels to stick together.

Step 3. The blood clots in a woven-net-like fashion. The net forms a plug that becomes a scab.

Once these life-saving measures have taken place, the next step is to stop infection.

Step 4. Now the blood vessels used initially to reduce the blood flow dilate to rush white blood cells to destroy any germs that entered in through the open wound. Then the body turns its attention to healing and rebuilding through a two-step process.

Step 5. New skin cells are formed at the site of the injury to fill the wound under the scab.

Step 6. Skin forming from one side of the injury meets with skin forming on the other sides of the injury to create a scar. The scar will grow stronger and began fading over several years.

Let's do a spiritual analysis of the process.

Step 1. The body comes together and controls the flow of news to the public. It doesn't matter what the world says (to a degree), but let it not be the body carrying out accusations against its own self. Do not allow the members of the body to hold open the wound causing the body to bleed out.

Step 2. Coming together to plug the infected area. This is not to say to condone the sin, but at this point, you don't even know the full story. If a brother or sister is family today and found in sin tomorrow, is he or she no longer family? Unless the Spirit leads differently, isn't our job at this point to reconcile them back to the sheepfold in love? Too often the only choice we give our brothers and sisters is to go back to the world, and then we talk about them for not coming to the church. It's kind of hard to go to a place where you've been kicked out.

Step 3. This is where we cover and cast a net of prayer, fasting, counsel, and so on over our brothers and sisters. If you can picture a net, spiritually it would look like the interjoining of these spiritual lines of communications (prayer, fasting, interceding) at multiple points keeping those things that need to be together, together, letting some things go, and allowing other things that need to come in, come in, as in accordance with Matt 18:18: "Verily I say unto you, Whatsoever ye shall bind on earth shall be bound in heaven: and whatsoever ye shall loose on earth shall be loosed in heaven." This net forms a scab and reminds us of the grace of God at work in our lives.

Step 4. The infusion of white blood cells. This is perhaps the most critical part of this reconciliation process because this is where the washing and cleansing takes place. The importance here is that in order for this step to take place, there must be an acceptance of culpability in the sin, then taking responsibility and submission to spiritual reconciliation. Humbling for anyone, especially of leadership. Only in the admission and ownership of the transgression can the remainder of the process go forth as stated in 1 John 1:9: "If we confess our sins, he is faithful and just to forgive us our sins, and to cleanse us from all unrighteousness." What makes this so critical is that this may be the decision point that makes the difference between surgically removed and surgically repaired. Although the scar will be visible, the healing and rebuilding process can now take place, and over time, even if the scar is still seen, its effect will not be.

Not to say that this revelation is all encompassing, but I believe it gives us a little insight as to how we should interact with each other as brothers and sisters (family) in the Lord. In its understanding, we see that we are not just together by the ideology that Christ is Lord. But in this revelation is also instruction on how we the members of this body repair, restore, and heal ourselves when wounded by the attacks of the enemy.

The same blood that flows at my elbow will eventually flow through my fingers. We are all connected by the same blood. The same blood that gives me life gives you life. We are family, brothers and sisters through the blood of Christ, which makes us blood relatives. It's a constant reminder that we have all suffered trauma (sin) and have fallen short of the glory of God.

The type of sin committed, the gifts, callings, titles and number of years saved doesn't make one better than another. We don't have the right to first cast a stone, because none of us is without trauma (sin), nor did he come to condemn the world, but that the world through him might be saved. The use of the word *trauma* is not to minimize the reality of sin or to give it a less harsh term that allows sin to be acceptable. It is just the means to make the analogy of what takes place in the spirit. And if we saw our brothers and sisters in Christ as our own bodies, maybe we'd think twice before we decided to destroy or amputate our member. We stab each other in the back and wonder why we walk funny. In the end, we all came from the same dirt.

Just because God commanded that we will return to the dust from which we came does not mean that dust is all that should be left of us. God gave us the power of the Holy Spirit to become the sons of God, power to impact and change lives. Don't leave here and the only thing that's left of you is dust.

I remember the Spirit telling me one time, "Don't be a thief on the cross."

I asked, "What did he mean by that?"

He said, "Don't accept me as your Lord and savior and the only thing you do after that is die and be with me in paradise. Don't rob the world of the glory of the gift by allowing it to only be a banner that we wear to say, 'I'm a Christian.' But let there be a path of righteousness, good works, and great exploits through the gifts that will lead the world to the cross."

Think about it like this. We have this treasure in earthen vessels, the gift of an all-powerful Holy Spirit. Why have that much power and be an ordinary human?

I remember a conversation I had with my pastor, and he said it just like this, "The son of a donkey is a donkey, and if we are the sons of God, then aren't we gods." I know that bothers some people, but just like the parable of the talents, God is expecting a return on the gifts that he has given. He gave us supernatural power through his Holy Spirit. Ordinary men don't raise the dead, touch and heal, speak life to a dead situation. God expects a supernatural return from a supernatural gift.

The power of the Holy Spirit to heal the sick, raise the dead, save from sin, stay the hand of death, and stop the forces of darkness is too much power to leave only a record of dust. So when the dust does settle, there should be a historical record of the power of God in the lives of those we left behind.

Chapter 6

EARTH'S AGE: THE SCIENCE OF CREATION

It is widely accepted that the time span from creation to the birth of Christ is approximately four thousand years. I have furniture that in its creation/manufacturing was created to look old, aged, or went under a strenuous aging process. That in itself is not evidence for my point, because looking old does not necessarily mean being old. The best we can do here on earth is make new look old. We do not have the creative power of God to make new old. Here is science and geologists understanding of the time it takes to create a mountain.

Science tells us that the earth is hundreds of millions, even billions, of years old, in part due to the time it takes to create landforms such as mountains. This estimate directly contradicts the Bible's six-day account of creation. Whether hundreds of millions or billions of years, science and the Bible will always be at odds. Mainly, according to science, it is impossible for land forms that take millions of years to form to be produced in just six days. The point is that God created earth with trees, grass, hills, and mountains in an instant, just by speaking. So what science says takes millions of years, God did in days.

Just like Adam wasn't created a baby—he was created a man. We know that on the seventh day, he was a day old, but we have no idea what age he was created. He was able to walk and talk, and he had knowledge far beyond a babe and many adults. So, if he can create something old brand-new, then no wonder science and creation are at odds with each other as it references time, and the reality may be that they're both right.

Science and our study of earth dates the earth as millions of years old because we understand the process and the time it takes to create the different land forms. So science may be right in the sense that we live on an earth that represents land forms that would take millions of years to form. They just didn't take into account an omnipotent God.

Science will never accept God, because it is only the spirit of God that reveals God. Not only can we not know him with our minds, but also we cannot serve him with our minds, and science can't wrap its mind around a God that has no beginning and has no end, is all powerful, all knowing, forever present, and everywhere at the same time. Their world is finite; it has a beginning and an end, and they can't conceive the infinite of God. Take a look at this timeline.

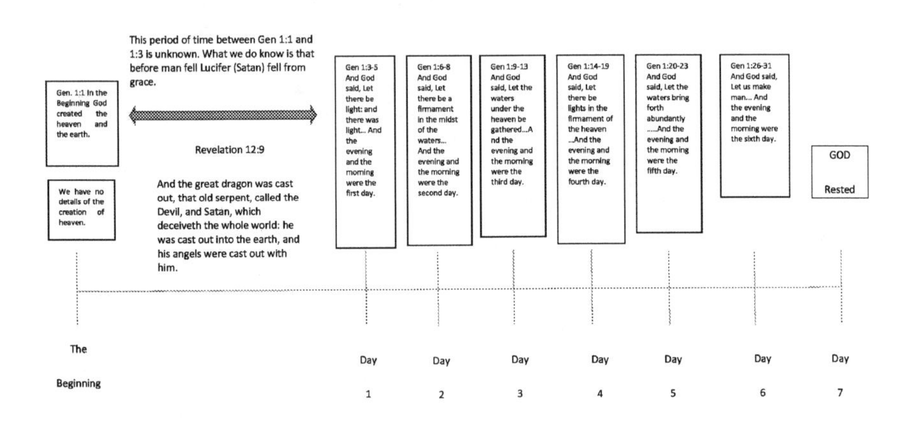

Therefore, we have an earth that was created in six days with characteristics of an earth that's millions of years old. The truth is it doesn't matter how old earth is. The question is, will you believe and serve God? Because we have two options for eternity and one way to heaven.

Chapter 7

GOD IS LOVE: IT'S ABOUT RIGHT, NOT YOUR FEELINGS

He that loveth not knoweth not God; for God is love.
—1 John 4:8

If love is the essence of God, then everything that he does, he does out of love. For many people, it's hard for them to wrap their minds around that, especially when some of the things he does or allows don't seem lovely. We have some belief that love agrees with or accepts everything, is submissive, has no standard, is not confrontational, obliges, and gives in, and when we see a demonstration that is in contrast to these beliefs, the first accusation we want to level at the would-be offender is "and you call yourself a Christian."

Love is powerful, and strong. It has a standard. It's uncompromising to its core. It's everything. In the Bible, 1 Corinthians 13 says, it is, it gives, and it takes, but most of all, it does what's best for the person, persons, or cause. In the case of righteousness and the events in the Bible that God performs/allows to get his people to a state of righteousness, it is sometimes ugly. I remember times when my parents would say as they chastised me with the rod of correction (not abusing me), "This hurts me more than it hurts you." I didn't understand that until I had children. The Bible says in Hebrews 12:6 and Revelation 3:19, "He chasteneth whom he loves." Some of God's chastening seems harsh and even unfair. It's this side of love that we find hard to accept.

Chapter 7

DO YOU REALLY LOVE HIM?

I'm not sure if the church at large understands the gravity of our call. The state of the church, the body of Christ, is one that I contemplate from time to time. My greatest concern is our perception or belief about Christianity versus what the Bible says.

The other day I overheard someone trying to console a relative about a loved one's Christianity. The conversation went something like this: "Just because he or she doesn't go to church or do this or that doesn't mean he or she doesn't love the Lord." It gave me great pause, because I hear these kinds of words often, especially at a funeral or when someone has passed: "He's in a better place now."

We want to make the family member who survives the deceased feel comforted about the person's now present state of being or the person who knows the truth about their loved one. We want to make them feel better about their relative who is a good person. After all, "prosperity, living well, and having a good or kind heart is a sign of God's blessing" or that we love God, so he or she must be ok. The real truth is that in today's society, no one goes to hell, and it would be rude to suggest otherwise to a grieving loved one. So some, for the sake of a loved one's feelings, give the impression that everyone is ok. We're all going to heaven.

It is not my place to judge. It is my place to give the word and let the hearer decide. So, instead of taking the word of someone who heard what someone else said about it, let's hear it from the source of the word himself. According to Deuteronomy 10:12, "And now, Israel, what doth the Lord thy God require of thee, but to fear the Lord thy God, to walk in all his ways, and to love him, and to serve the Lord thy God with all thy heart and with all thy soul."

Without going into a long dissertation, to "love the Lord" is a requirement and to do so with all one's heart and soul: pretty straightforward and self-explanatory, although the degree of "all one's heart and soul" can be interpreted in many ways. Deuteronomy 13:3 states, "Thou shalt not hearken unto the words of that prophet, or that dreamer of dreams: for the Lord your God proveth you, to know whether ye love the Lord your God with all your heart and with all your soul. In this verse it says, man is not going to be able to define your love for God for you, God will test you to prove to you if you love him or not."

In the following scriptures in John 14, the word himself defines whether or not you love him. John 14:14 says, "If ye love me, keep my commandments." John 14:21 says, "He that hath my commandments, and keepeth them, he it is that loveth me: and he that loveth me shall be loved of my Father, and I will love him, and will manifest myself to him." John 14:23–24 continues, "Jesus answered and said unto him, 'If a man love me, he will keep my words: and my Father will love him, and we will come unto him, and make our abode with him. He that loveth me not keepeth not my sayings: and the word which ye hear is not mine, but the Father's which sent me.'"

These words spoken by Jesus himself need no further explanation. Going to church, being a "good" person, for our "good" is as filthy rags, having a kind heart, caring about people, all sound good, even sound as though they qualify, but they don't. This is my take on it: love requires consideration. What do I mean by that? The person(s) that I love is in my thoughts always. What I say, how I say, when I'm in the grocery store, I think about what they would like to eat. When I'm shopping, I think about what I would like to give them. I could see something nice, and it would remind me of them. I'm constantly considering them. They are not a footnote or an afterthought. I don't do it to get points. I don't do it for them to do for me later. I am intentional in my walk, talk, and thoughts. I consider them before I act, and I act based on them. My love for them drives and guides my life. They own me because they have my heart.

Chapter 9

THIS IS YOUR FAITH

This word of God is your faith. The just shall live by it. You should know it for yourself. It has been my observation that most of what the church at large knows about the Bible has been told to them. There are many members of our congregations who have Bibles, even fewer who read on any consistent basis, and far less who are students of the word. I constantly hear misquotes of the Bible and the interpretation thereof. The real concern is there is a large population that is repeating the same misquote and interpretation.

I am convinced that if you don't know your God, you will accept anyone's version of him. Simply stated, if you don't know your Bible, you're almost forced, even required, to accept the version given to you. After all, what will your counterversion or opinion be, if you don't have one for yourself, if you don't indeed own your own God?

Here we're going to bring some of those misquotes and interpretations to light.

"The race isn't given to the swift or the strong, but to him who endures to the end." This is not per se an inaccurate statement, just that it's not a quote from the Bible as I had been led to believe nearly all of my church life. This may very well be a mostly African American misquote of the Bible. I've heard teachings on it, preaching on it, testimonies of it, and even songs. I remember the first time

I told the church in a Bible study that it wasn't in the Bible, one of the young ministers literally spent a good deal of the Bible study frantically searching for it. When I first said it, he did a beeline to his Bible, flipping through pages and the concordance with all confidence that he would find it. As the Bible study went on, you could see the look of despair and defeat on his face, and it was ok, because getting it right meant enough to him to search for it.

The misquote is actually a combination of two scriptures: Ecclesiastes 9:11 and Matthew 10:22. They read as follows: "I returned, and saw under the sun, that the race is not to the swift, nor the battle to the strong, neither yet bread to the wise, nor yet riches to men of understanding, nor yet favour to men of skill; but time and chance happeneth to them all" (Ecclesiastes 9:11). "And ye shall be hated of all men for my name's sake; but he that endureth to the end shall be saved (Matthew 10:22).

How about this one? "The grace of God won't take you where it won't keep or protect you." This is not a false statement; it's just that most interpretations of this is it's a safety scripture with the belief that nothing will hurt or harm me. We are led as sheep to the slaughter. Look at the persecution of the disciples, even the death of the cross. Surely the grace of God can keep us in all things, but don't be surprised if you make it to heaven before you planned, because it may just cost you your life. Me, personally, I take the Hebrew boys' point of view: "Even if he doesn't deliver me from this, he is able." We were chosen in the furnace of affliction. Matthew 13:21 says that tribulation and persecution ariseth because of the word. We should expect persecution and know that "to live is Christ, and to die is gain." This is how I see it, "To Live is Christ and to die is Christ."

This one I hear more often than I care to: "All you need is a little faith." That's the scripture used so that one can feel comfortable with barely believing God. Because they refer to "little faith" in comparison to "a grain of mustard seed." You will find references of this grain of mustard seed in Matthew 13:31, 17:20, Mark 4:31, and Luke 13:19 and 17:6. In Matthew 13 and Mark 31, the takeaway is not the connotation of a grain being small, but how potent our faith (the word of God) is and the results it brings.

Take, for example, Mark 4:31. If that is the only scripture you quote to justify "only needing little faith," you will miss the entire lesson. Continue to the thirty-second verse and then you will know what true faith is, but taken out of context, you will be led to believe that little faith is all God requires of you. If you would research the mustard seed, you will find that it is a plant that should be planted in the garden, but because if grows so large, it's planted, as one resource states it, in the groves amongst the trees. I heard a preacher say the Bible is God's brag book. He didn't brag about little things; he bragged about big things. Little faith only shows the world we have a little God.

Finally, look at what Jesus said. There are four passages in the New Testament where Jesus uses the phrase "o ye of little faith." That was not Jesus's resounding approval of little faith. Indeed, it was more of a reprimand. God wants to blow the world's mind with your faith. As Jesus often said, "According to your faith, be it unto you." So you must decide whether the world sees the great big God that he is or the cliché of "just a little God."

Another misquote is that I must decrease that God/Christ increase. Let's see how the scripture reads. John 3:30 says, "He must increase, but I must decrease." This is the illustration that I did to explain this scripture. I took a basket that was filled with different items and first read it the misquoted way. If I decrease—so I took items out of the basket representing me decreasing, then I said, "If I decrease by taking things out, I can replace it with anything, but if, quoting the scripture correctly, Christ increases, then he will, as he increases, push anything that is not like him out. It's an automatic response—those things have no choice but to leave until the only thing that's left is Christ.

Some people say this is splitting hairs and it's being too critical. But what if you were on the operating table and the surgeon was to make a hairline incision barely seen by the naked eye, but instead made an indiscriminate cut as to say any size opening is ok, would it matter then? But it's not that serious. It's more than that serious. Someone's eternity is hanging in the balance of the words you speak. This word is not just my faith; it's my life and my eternity. I think that makes it important enough at least to me to know it.

In a Sunday school lesson, I started with asking the congregation if they heard the recent news about a celebrity and some had. Then I asked what was the theme for the study for the month, and they couldn't tell me. I once read that you can name a worldly song in the church and a great majority of the congregants know it by heart, but when it comes to a gospel or Christian song, you have to put the words on the screen.

It's a sad commentary, but the word of God is going to have to be relevant in the house of God. At least in God's house, his word should carry some weight.

Thine, O LORD, is the greatness, and the power, and the glory, and the victory, and the majesty: for all that is in the heaven and in the earth is thine; thine is the kingdom, O LORD, and thou art exalted as head above all.

Both riches and honour come of thee, and thou reignest over all; and in thine hand is power and might; and in thine hand it is to make great, and to give strength unto all.

Now therefore, our God, we thank thee, and praise thy glorious name.

But who am I, and what is my people, that we should be able to offer so willingly after this sort? for all things come of thee, and of thine own have we given thee. I Chron 29:11-14 (KJV)

Everyone is a Christian. For some reason holiness doesn't seem to be a requirement for Christianity. We are more concerned about not upsetting the apple cart, not calling sin, sin. It sounds better, easier to digest, if we call it a mistake. It seems we don't really teach holiness. We just want our members to live well, live good lives, have good jobs and a decent standard of living. We want them to be moral and ethical. News flash, I'm sorry, but God requires holiness, and he defines what is or is not holy. He didn't ask us to be moral or ethical (by man's standards), nor did he tell us to give our allegiance to anything other than the spirit of God. We are quick to follow the flavor of the day or lend our ear to the sound that aligns with our individual tint. The word of God and the Holy Spirit must be our filter; it can't be what's popular, what's easy, or what makes us comfortable.

If you're going to be at the marriage supper, you're going to have to be holy. God will not be joined with sin or unrighteousness. If He turned away from his son, turned his back on him, forsook him while on the cross, his only begotten son, not because he sinned, but simply because he bore the sins of the world at that time. If he turned away from his son in his obedience to shoulder the sins of the world, what makes you think he will pollute himself with a bride who is sinful by choice.

God does things with the end in mind, and too often we only think of the moment. I believe that we sometimes forget we are spirit beings living in a temporary shell and, therefore, make too many decisions based on our temporary status without realizing they have eternal implications. If we make everlasting decisions thinking only of today or our current situations, we will be unprepared for tomorrow's spiritual realities. The word says that for the joy that was set before him, he went to the cross. He couldn't afford to think about what was happening to him at the moment. He was looking into eternity, so he made his decisions based on the end and not the moment.

Decisions of faith are not to be made based on the situation but based on obedience to faith alone. Because faith has a destiny, and it's not in the situation. It's in the end of the situation. It works through the situation and helps you along the way, but its destiny and outcome is in the end, because that's how God operates. He does not start unless he has already finished. Isaiah 46:10 says, "He declares the end from the beginning." He doesn't figure it out along the way. Faith in and of itself does not consider obstacles, not that it is not aware of them, but it does not make decisions based on them and only proclaims its desire—what we call in the military in conducting an operation *the end state.*

As long as you make decisions based on situations, you haven't seen faith's end, and you will fall short of faith's destiny. In Ecclesiastes 11:4, the Bible says, "He who observeth the rain will not plant and he who regardeth the cloud will not reap." We find ourselves struggling and fighting in the middle of faith, because for so many of us that's as far as we are able to see ourselves, at the obstacle. And it's at the obstacles many of us live our lives.

What if God said, "I won't love because man will sin or man will hate"? What if you said, "I won't look for a job, because someone will turn me down or won't hire me"? We continue putting in applications because the end state of receiving a job is worth the disappointments and struggles of every hiring manager's decision not to select you as his or her choice.

When Adam sinned he broke the marriage bond between God and man, and because God cannot cohabitate with sin, the only way to get his bride back was to buy her back. If you do not believe on him, then you don't believe on his sacrifice, and if you don't believe on his sacrifice, you have no way to connect or commune with him—you can't partake in the marriage supper.

I hope you don't expect for there to be a section of unbelievers at the marriage supper, sitting or eating by themselves, because the parting or separating will have already taken place. This will be the true body of Christ. Everyone whose name is on a church roll won't be there. Contrary to popular belief, it is not a ticket to heaven.

Some people ask the question, why would God create Adam and Eve, knowing they were going to sin? Because he wasn't looking at

Printed in the United States
By Bookmasters